INDIAN COOKBOOK 2021

FLAVORFUL INDIAN RECIPES

JANE PETERSON

Table of Contents

No-Oil Chicken

Serves 4

Ingredients

400g/14oz yoghurt

1 tsp chilli powder

1 tsp ginger paste

1 tsp garlic paste

2 green chillies, finely chopped

50g/1¾oz coriander leaves, ground

1 tsp garam masala

Salt to taste

750g/1lb 10oz boneless chicken, chopped into 8 pieces

Method

- Mix together all the ingredients, except the chicken. Marinate the chicken with this mixture overnight.

- Cook the marinated chicken in a saucepan on a medium heat for 40 minutes, stirring frequently. Serve hot.

Kozi Varatha Curry

(Kairali Chicken Curry from Kerala)

Serves 4

Ingredients

60ml/2fl oz refined vegetable oil

7.5cm/3in root ginger, finely chopped

15 garlic cloves, finely chopped

8 shallots, sliced

3 green chillies, slit lengthways

1kg/2¼lb chicken, chopped into 12 pieces

¾ tsp turmeric

Salt to taste

2 tbsp ground coriander

1 tbsp garam masala

½ tsp cumin seeds

750ml/1¼ pints coconut milk

5-6 curry leaves

Method

- Heat the oil in a saucepan. Add the ginger and garlic. Fry on a medium heat for 30 seconds.

- Add the shallots and green chillies. Stir-fry for a minute.

- Add the chicken, turmeric, salt, ground coriander, garam masala and cumin seeds. Mix well. Cover with a lid and cook on a low heat for 20 minutes. Add the coconut milk. Simmer for 20 minutes.

- Garnish with the curry leaves and serve hot.

Chicken Stew

Ingredients

1 tbsp refined vegetable oil

2 cloves

2.5cm/1in cinnamon

6 black peppercorns

3 bay leaves

2 large onions, chopped into 8 pieces

1 tsp ginger paste

1 tsp garlic paste

8 chicken drumsticks

200g/7oz frozen mixed vegetables

250ml/8fl oz water

Salt to taste

2 tsp plain white flour, dissolved in 360ml/12fl oz milk

Method

- Heat the oil in a saucepan. Add the cloves, cinnamon, peppercorns and bay leaves. Let them splutter for 30 seconds.

- Add the onions, ginger paste and garlic paste. Fry for 2 minutes.

- Add the remaining ingredients, except the flour mixture. Cover with a lid and simmer for 30 minutes. Add the flour mixture. Mix well.

- Simmer for 10 minutes, stirring frequently. Serve hot.

Chicken Himani

(Cardamom Chicken)

Serves 4

Ingredients

1kg/2¼lb chicken, chopped into 10 pieces

3 tbsp refined vegetable oil

¼ tsp ground green cardamom

Salt to taste

For the marinade:

1 tsp ginger paste

1 tsp garlic paste

200g/7oz yoghurt

2 tbsp mint leaves, ground

Method

- Mix all the marinade ingredients together. Marinate the chicken with this mixture for 4 hours.

- Heat the oil in a saucepan. Add the marinated chicken and fry on a low heat for 10 minutes. Add the cardamom and salt. Mix well and cook for 30 minutes, stirring frequently. Serve hot.

White Chicken

Ingredients

750g/1lb 10oz boneless chicken, chopped

1 tsp ginger paste

1 tsp garlic paste

1 tbsp ghee

2 cloves

2.5cm/1in cinnamon

8 black peppercorns

2 bay leaves

Salt to taste

250ml/8fl oz water

30g/1oz cashew nuts, ground

10-12 almonds, ground

1 tbsp single cream

Method

- Marinate the chicken with the ginger paste and garlic paste for 30 minutes.

- Heat the ghee in a saucepan. Add the cloves, cinnamon, peppercorns, bay leaves and salt. Let them splutter for 15 seconds.

- Add the marinated chicken and water. Simmer for 30 minutes. Add the cashew nuts, almonds and cream. Cook for 5 minutes and serve hot.

Chicken in Red Masala

Serves 4

Ingredients

3 tbsp refined vegetable oil

2 large onions, finely sliced

1 tbsp poppy seeds

5 dry red chillies

50g/1¾oz fresh coconut, grated

2.5cm/1in cinnamon

2 tsp tamarind paste

6 garlic cloves

500g/1lb 2oz chicken, chopped

2 tomatoes, finely sliced

1 tbsp ground coriander

1 tsp ground cumin

500ml/16fl oz water

Salt to taste

Method

- Heat the oil in a saucepan. Fry the onions on a medium heat till brown. Add the poppy seeds, chillies, coconut and cinnamon. Fry for 3 minutes.

- Add the tamarind paste and garlic. Mix well and grind into a paste.

- Mix this paste with all the remaining ingredients. Cook the mixture in a saucepan on a low heat for 40 minutes. Serve hot.

Chicken Jhalfrezie

(Chicken in Thick Tomato Gravy)

Serves 4

Ingredients

3 tbsp refined vegetable oil

3 large onions, finely chopped

2.5cm/1in root ginger, finely sliced

1 tsp garlic paste

1kg/2¼lb chicken, chopped into 8 pieces

½ tsp turmeric

3 tsp ground coriander

1 tsp ground cumin

4 tomatoes, blanched and puréed

Salt to taste

Method

- Heat the oil in a saucepan. Add the onions, ginger and garlic paste. Fry on a medium heat till the onions are brown.

- Add the chicken, turmeric, ground coriander and ground cumin. Fry for 5 minutes.

- Add the tomato purée and salt. Mix well and cook on a low heat for 40 minutes, stirring occasionally. Serve hot.

Simple Chicken Curry

Serves 4

Ingredients

2 tbsp refined vegetable oil

2 large onions, sliced

½ tsp turmeric

1 tsp ginger paste

1 tsp garlic paste

6 green chillies, sliced

750g/1lb 10oz chicken, chopped into 8 pieces

125g/4½oz yoghurt

125g/4½oz khoya*

Salt to taste

50g/1¾oz coriander leaves, finely chopped

Method

- Heat the oil in a saucepan. Add the onions. Fry till they turn translucent.

- Add the turmeric, ginger paste, garlic paste and green chillies. Fry on a medium heat for 2 minutes. Add the chicken and fry for 5 minutes.

- Add the yoghurt, khoya and salt. Mix thoroughly. Cover with a lid and cook on a low heat for 30 minutes, stirring occasionally.

- Garnish with the coriander leaves. Serve hot.

Sour Chicken Curry

Serves 4

Ingredients

1kg/2¼lb chicken, chopped into 8 pieces

Salt to taste

½ tsp turmeric

4 tbsp refined vegetable oil

3 onions, finely chopped

8 curry leaves

3 tomatoes, finely chopped

1 tsp ginger paste

1 tsp garlic paste

1 tbsp ground coriander

1 tsp garam masala

1 tbsp tamarind paste

½ tbsp ground black pepper

250ml/8fl oz water

Method

- Marinate the chicken pieces with the salt and turmeric for 30 minutes.

- Heat the oil in a saucepan. Add the onions and curry leaves. Fry on a low heat till the onions are translucent.

- Add all the remaining ingredients and the marinated chicken. Mix well, cover with a lid and simmer for 40 minutes. Serve hot.

Anjeer Dry Chicken

(Dry Chicken with Figs)

Serves 4

Ingredients

750g/1lb 10oz chicken, chopped into 12 pieces

4 tbsp ghee

2 large onions, finely chopped

250ml/8fl oz water

Salt to taste

For the marinade:

10 dry figs, soaked for 1 hour

1 tsp ginger paste

1 tsp garlic paste

200g/7oz yoghurt

1½ tsp garam masala

2 tbsp single cream

Method

- Mix all the marinade ingredients together. Marinate the chicken with this mixture for an hour.

- Heat the ghee in a saucepan. Fry the onions on a medium heat till brown.

- Add the marinated chicken, water and salt. Mix well, cover with a lid and simmer for 40 minutes. Serve hot.

Chicken Yoghurt

Serves 4

Ingredients

30g/1oz mint leaves, finely chopped

30g/1oz coriander leaves, chopped

2 tsp ginger paste

2 tsp garlic paste

400g/14oz yoghurt

200g/7oz tomato purée

Juice of 1 lemon

1kg/2¼lb chicken, chopped into 12 pieces

2 tbsp refined vegetable oil

4 large onions, finely chopped

Salt to taste

Method

- Grind the mint leaves and coriander leaves to a fine paste. Mix this with the ginger paste, garlic paste, yoghurt, tomato purée and lemon juice. Marinate the chicken with this mixture for 3 hours.

- Heat the oil in a saucepan. Fry the onions on a medium heat till brown.

- Add the marinated chicken. Cover with a lid and simmer for 40 minutes, stirring occasionally. Serve hot.

Spicy Fried Chicken

Serves 4

Ingredients

1 tsp ginger paste

2 tsp garlic paste

2 green chillies, finely chopped

1 tsp chilli powder

1 tsp garam masala

2 tsp lemon juice

½ tsp turmeric

Salt to taste

1kg/2¼lb chicken, chopped into 8 pieces

Refined vegetable oil for deep-frying

Breadcrumbs, to coat

Method

- Mix the ginger paste, garlic paste, green chillies, chilli powder, garam masala, lemon juice, turmeric and salt together. Marinate the chicken with this mixture for 3 hours.

- Heat the oil in a frying pan. Coat each marinated chicken piece with the breadcrumbs and deep fry on a medium heat till golden brown.

- Drain on absorbent paper and serve hot.

Chicken Supreme

Serves 4

Ingredients

1 tsp ginger paste

1 tsp garlic paste

1kg/2¼lb chicken, chopped into 8 pieces

200g/7oz yoghurt

Salt to taste

250ml/8fl oz water

2 tbsp refined vegetable oil

2 large onions, sliced

4 red chillies

5cm/2in cinnamon

2 black cardamom pods

4 cloves

1 tbsp chana dhal*, dry roasted

Method

- Mix the ginger paste and garlic paste together. Marinate the chicken with this mixture for 30 minutes. Add the yoghurt, salt and water. Set aside.

- Heat the oil in a saucepan. Add the onions, chillies, cinnamon, cardamom, cloves and chana dhal. Fry for 3-4 minutes on a low heat.

- Grind to a paste and add to the chicken mixture. Mix well.

- Cook on a low heat for 30 minutes. Serve hot.

Chicken Vindaloo

(Spicy Goan-style Chicken Curry)

Serves 4

Ingredients

60ml/2fl oz malt vinegar

1 tbsp cumin seeds

1 tsp peppercorns

6 red chillies

1 tsp turmeric

Salt to taste

4 tbsp refined vegetable oil

3 large onions, finely chopped

1kg/2¼lb chicken, chopped into 8 pieces

Method

- Grind the vinegar with the cumin seeds, peppercorns, chillies, turmeric and salt to a smooth paste. Set aside.

- Heat the oil in a saucepan. Add the onions and fry till translucent. Add the vinegar-cumin seeds paste. Mix well and fry for 4-5 minutes.

- Add the chicken and cook on a low heat for 30 minutes. Serve hot.

Caramelized Chicken

Serves 4

Ingredients

200g/7oz yoghurt

1 tsp ginger paste

1 tsp garlic paste

2 tbsp ground coriander

1 tsp ground cumin

1½ tsp garam masala

Salt to taste

1kg/2¼lb chicken, chopped into 8 pieces

3 tbsp refined vegetable oil

2 tsp sugar

3 cloves

2.5cm/1in cinnamon

6 black peppercorns

Method

- Mix together the yoghurt, ginger paste, garlic paste, ground coriander, ground cumin, garam masala and salt. Marinate the chicken with this mixture overnight.

- Heat the oil in a saucepan. Add the sugar, cloves, cinnamon and peppercorns. Fry for a minute. Add the marinated chicken and cook on a low heat for 40 minutes. Serve hot.

Cashew Chicken

Serves 4

Ingredients

1kg/2¼lb chicken, chopped into 12 pieces

Salt to taste

1 tsp ginger paste

1 tsp garlic paste

4 tbsp refined vegetable oil

4 large onions, sliced

15 cashew nuts, ground to a paste

6 red chillies, soaked for 15 minutes

2 tsp ground cumin

60ml/2fl oz ketchup

500ml/16fl oz water

Method

- Marinate the chicken with the salt and ginger and garlic pastes for 1 hour.

- Heat the oil in a saucepan. Fry the onions on a medium heat till brown.

- Add the cashew nuts, chillies, cumin and ketchup. Cook for 5 minutes.

- Add the chicken and the water. Simmer for 40 minutes and serve hot.

Quick Chicken

Ingredients

4 tbsp refined vegetable oil

6 red chillies

6 black peppercorns

1 tsp coriander seeds

1 tsp cumin seeds

2.5cm/1in cinnamon

4 cloves

1 tsp turmeric

8 garlic cloves

1 tsp tamarind paste

4 medium-sized onions, finely sliced

2 large tomatoes, finely chopped

1kg/2¼lb chicken, chopped into 12 pieces

250ml/8fl oz water

Salt to taste

Method

- Heat half a tbsp of oil in a saucepan. Add the red chillies, peppercorns, coriander seeds, cumin seeds, cinnamon and cloves. Fry them on a medium heat for 2-3 minutes.
- Add the turmeric, garlic and tamarind paste. Grind the mixture to a smooth paste. Set aside.
- Heat the remaining oil in a saucepan. Add the onions and fry them on a medium heat till they are brown. Add the tomatoes and sauté for 3-4 minutes.
- Add the chicken and sauté for 4-5 minutes.
- Add the water and salt. Mix well and cover with a lid. Simmer for 40 minutes, stirring occasionally.
- Serve hot.

Coorgi Chicken Curry

Serves 4

Ingredients

1kg/2¼lb chicken, chopped into 12 pieces

Salt to taste

1 tsp turmeric

50g/1¾oz grated coconut

3 tbsp refined vegetable oil

1 tsp garlic paste

2 large onions, finely sliced

1 tsp ground cumin

1 tsp ground coriander

360ml/12fl oz water

Method

- Marinate the chicken with the salt and turmeric for an hour. Set aside.
- Grind the coconut with enough water to form a smooth paste.
- Heat the oil in a saucepan. Add the coconut paste with the garlic paste, onions, ground cumin and coriander. Fry on a low heat for 4-5 minutes.
- Add the marinated chicken. Mix well and fry for 4-5 minutes. Add the water, cover with a lid and simmer for 40 minutes. Serve hot.

Pan Chicken

Serves 4

Ingredients

4 tbsp refined vegetable oil

1 tsp ginger paste

1 tsp garlic paste

2 large onions, finely chopped

1 tsp garam masala

1½ tbsp cashew nuts, ground

1½ tbsp melon seeds*, ground

1 tsp ground coriander

500g/1lb 2oz boneless chicken

200g/7oz tomato purée

2 chicken stock cubes

250ml/8fl oz water

Salt to taste

Method

- Heat the oil in a saucepan. Add the ginger paste, garlic paste, onions and garam masala. Fry for 2-3 minutes on a low heat. Add the cashew nuts, melon seeds and ground coriander. Fry for 2 minutes.
- Add the chicken and fry for 5 minutes. Add the tomato purée, stock cubes, water and salt. Cover and simmer for 40 minutes. Serve hot.

Spinach Chicken

Ingredients

3 tbsp refined vegetable oil

6 cloves

5cm/2in cinnamon

2 bay leaves

2 large onions, finely chopped

12 garlic cloves, finely chopped

400g/14oz spinach, coarsely chopped

200g/7oz yoghurt

250ml/8fl oz water

750g/1lb 10oz chicken, chopped into 8 pieces

Salt to taste

Method

- Heat 2 tbsp oil in a saucepan. Add the cloves, cinnamon and bay leaves. Let them splutter for 15 seconds.
- Add the onions and fry them on a medium heat till they turn translucent.
- Add the garlic and spinach. Mix well. Cook for 5-6 minutes. Cool and grind with enough water to make a smooth paste.
- Heat the remaining oil in a saucepan. Add the spinach paste and fry for 3-4 minutes. Add the yoghurt and water. Cook for 5-6 minutes. Add the chicken and salt. Cook on a low heat for 40 minutes. Serve hot.

Chicken Indienne

Serves 4

Ingredients

4-5 tbsp refined vegetable oil

4 large onions, minced

1kg/2¼lb chicken, chopped into 10 pieces

Salt to taste

500ml/16fl oz water

For the spice mixture:

2.5cm/1in root ginger

10 garlic cloves

1 tbsp garam masala

2 tsp fennel seeds

1½ tbsp coriander seeds

60ml/2fl oz water

Method

- Grind the spice mixture ingredients into a smooth paste. Set aside.
- Heat the oil in a saucepan. Fry the onions on a medium heat till brown.
- Add the spice mixture paste, the chicken and salt. Fry for 5-6 minutes. Add the water. Cover and cook for 40 minutes. Serve hot.

Kori Gassi

(Mangalorean Chicken with Curry)

Serves 4

Ingredients

4 tbsp refined vegetable oil

6 whole red chillies

1 tsp black peppercorns

4 tsp coriander seeds

2 tsp cumin seeds

150g/5½oz fresh coconut, grated

8 garlic cloves

500ml/16fl oz water

3 large onions, finely chopped

1 tsp turmeric

1kg/2¼lb chicken, chopped into 8 pieces

2 tsp tamarind paste

Salt to taste

Method

- Heat 1 tsp oil in a saucepan. Add the red chillies, peppercorns, coriander seeds and cumin seeds. Let them splutter for 15 seconds.
- Grind this mixture to a paste with the coconut, garlic and half the water.
- Heat the remaining oil in a saucepan. Add the onions, turmeric and the coconut paste. Fry on a medium heat for 5-6 minutes.
- Add the chicken, tamarind paste, salt and the remaining water. Mix well. Cover with a lid and simmer for 40 minutes. Serve hot.

Chicken Ghezado

(Goan-style Chicken)

Serves 4

Ingredients

3 tbsp refined vegetable oil

2 large onions, finely chopped

1 tsp ginger paste

1 tsp garlic paste

2 tomatoes, finely chopped

1kg/2¼lb chicken, chopped into 8 pieces

1 tbsp ground coriander

2 tbsp garam masala

Salt to taste

250ml/8fl oz water

Method

- Heat the oil in a saucepan. Add the onions, ginger paste and garlic paste. Fry for 2 minutes. Add the tomatoes and chicken. Fry for 5 minutes.
- Add all the remaining ingredients. Simmer for 40 minutes and serve hot.

Chicken in Tomato Gravy

Serves 4

Ingredients

1 tbsp ghee

2.5cm/1in root ginger, finely chopped

10 garlic cloves, finely chopped

2 large onions, finely chopped

4 red chillies

1 tsp garam masala

1 tsp turmeric

800g/1¾lb tomato purée

1kg/2¼lb chicken, chopped into 8 pieces

Salt to taste

200g/7oz yoghurt

Method

- Heat the ghee in a saucepan. Add the ginger, garlic, onions, red chillies, garam masala and turmeric. Fry on a medium heat for 3 minutes.
- Add the tomato purée and fry for 4 minutes on a low heat.
- Add the chicken, salt and yoghurt. Mix thoroughly.
- Cover and simmer for 40 minutes, stirring occasionally. Serve hot.

Shahenshah Murgh

(Chicken cooked in Special Gravy)

Serves 4

Ingredients

250g/9oz peanuts, soaked for 4 hours

60g/2oz raisins

4 green chillies, slit lengthways

1 tbsp cumin seeds

4 tbsp ghee

1 tbsp ground cinnamon

3 large onions, finely chopped

1kg/2¼lb chicken, chopped in 12 pieces

Salt to taste

Method

- Drain the peanuts and grind them with the raisins, green chillies, cumin seeds and enough water to form a smooth paste. Set aside.
- Heat the ghee in a saucepan. Add the ground cinnamon. Let it splutter for 30 seconds.
- Add the onions and the ground peanut-raisin paste. Fry for 2-3 minutes.
- Add the chicken and salt. Mix well. Cook on a low heat for 40 minutes, stirring occasionally. Serve hot.

Chicken do Pyaaza

(Chicken with Onions)

Serves 4

Ingredients

4 tbsp ghee plus extra for deep frying

4 cloves

½ tsp fennel seeds

1 tsp ground coriander

1 tsp ground black pepper

2.5cm/1in root ginger, finely chopped

8 garlic cloves, finely chopped

4 large onions, sliced

1kg/2¼lb chicken, chopped into 12 pieces

½ tsp turmeric

4 tomatoes, finely chopped

Salt to taste

Method

- Heat 4 tbsp ghee in a saucepan. Add the cloves, fennel seeds, ground coriander and pepper. Let them splutter for 15 seconds.

- Add the ginger, garlic and onions. Fry on a medium heat for 1-2 minutes.

- Add the chicken, turmeric, tomatoes and salt. Mix well. Cook on a low heat for 30 minutes, stirring frequently. Serve hot.

Bengali Chicken

Serves 4

Ingredients

300g/10oz yoghurt

1 tsp ginger paste

1 tsp garlic paste

3 large onions, 1 grated plus 2 finely chopped

1 tsp turmeric

2 tsp chilli powder

Salt to taste

1kg/2¼lb chicken, chopped into 12 pieces

4 tbsp mustard oil

500ml/16fl oz water

Method

- Mix the yoghurt, ginger paste, garlic paste, onion, turmeric, chilli powder and salt together. Marinate the chicken with this mixture for 30 minutes.
- Heat the oil in a saucepan. Add the chopped onions and fry till brown.
- Add the marinated chicken, water and salt. Mix well. Cover with a lid and simmer for 40 minutes. Serve hot.

Lasooni Murgh

(Chicken cooked with Garlic)

Serves 4

Ingredients

200g/7oz yoghurt

2 tbsp garlic paste

1 tsp garam masala

2 tbsp lemon juice

1 tsp ground black pepper

5 saffron strands

Salt to taste

750g/1lb 10oz boneless chicken, chopped into 8 pieces

2 tbsp refined vegetable oil

60ml/2fl oz double cream

Method

- Mix together the yoghurt, garlic paste, garam masala, lemon juice, pepper, saffron, salt and chicken. Refrigerate the mixture overnight.
- Heat the oil in a saucepan. Add the chicken mixture, cover with a lid and cook on a low heat for 40 minutes, stirring occasionally.
- Add the cream and stir for a minute. Serve hot.

Chicken Cafreal

(Goan Chicken in a Coriander Sauce)

Serves 4

Ingredients

1kg/2¼lb chicken, chopped into 8 pieces

5 tbsp refined vegetable oil

250ml/8fl oz water

Salt to taste

4 lemons, quartered

For the marinade:

50g/1¾oz coriander leaves, chopped

2.5cm/1in root ginger

10 garlic cloves

120ml/4fl oz malt vinegar

1 tbsp garam masala

Method

- Mix all the marinade ingredients together and grind with enough water to form a smooth paste. Marinate the chicken with this mixture for an hour.

- Heat the oil in a saucepan. Add the marinated chicken and fry on a medium heat for 5 minutes. Add the water and salt. Cover with a lid and simmer for 40 minutes, stirring occasionally. Serve hot with the lemons.

Chicken with Apricots

Serves 4

Ingredients

4 tbsp refined vegetable oil

3 large onions, finely sliced

1 tsp ginger paste

1 tsp garlic paste

1kg/2¼lb chicken, chopped into 8 pieces

1 tsp chilli powder

1 tsp turmeric

2 tsp ground cumin

2 tbsp sugar

300g/10oz dried apricots, soaked for 10 minutes

60ml/2fl oz water

1 tbsp malt vinegar

Salt to taste

Method

- Heat the oil in a saucepan. Add the onions, ginger paste and garlic paste. Fry on a medium heat till the onions are brown.
- Add the chicken, chilli powder, turmeric, ground cumin and sugar. Mix well and fry for 5-6 minutes.
- Add the remaining ingredients. Simmer for 40 minutes and serve hot.

Grilled Chicken

Serves 4

Ingredients

Salt to taste

1 tbsp malt vinegar

1 tsp ground black pepper

1 tsp ginger paste

1 tsp garlic paste

2 tsp garam masala

1kg/2¼lb chicken, chopped into 8 pieces

2 tbsp ghee

2 large onions, sliced

2 tomatoes, finely chopped

Method

- Mix the salt, vinegar, pepper, ginger paste, garlic paste and garam masala together. Marinate the chicken with this mixture for an hour.

- Heat the ghee in a saucepan. Add the onions and fry on a medium heat till they turn brown.

- Add the tomatoes and marinated chicken. Mix thoroughly and fry for 4-5 minutes.

- Remove from the heat and grill the mixture for 40 minutes. Serve hot.

Pepper Duck Roast

Ingredients

2 tbsp malt vinegar

1½ tsp ginger paste

1 tsp garlic paste

Salt to taste

1 tsp ground black pepper

1kg/2¼lb duck

2 tbsp butter

2 tbsp refined vegetable oil

3 large onions, finely sliced

4 tomatoes, finely chopped

1 tsp sugar

500ml/16fl oz water

Method

- Mix the vinegar, ginger paste, garlic paste, salt and pepper. Pierce the duck with a fork and marinate with this mixture for 1 hour.

- Heat the butter and oil together in a saucepan. Add the onions and tomatoes. Fry on a medium heat for 3-4 minutes. Add the duck, sugar and water. Mix well and simmer for 45 minutes. Serve hot.

Bhuna Chicken

(Chicken cooked in Yoghurt)

Serves 4

Ingredients

4 tbsp refined vegetable oil

1kg/2¼lb chicken, chopped into 12 pieces

1 tsp ginger paste

1 tsp garlic paste

½ tsp turmeric

2 large onions, finely chopped

1½ tsp garam masala

1 tsp freshly ground black pepper

150g/5½oz yoghurt, whisked

Salt to taste

Method

- Heat the oil in a saucepan. Add the chicken and fry on a medium heat for 6-7 minutes. Drain and set aside.
- To the same oil, add the ginger paste, garlic paste, turmeric and onions. Fry on a medium heat for 2 minutes, stirring frequently.
- Add the fried chicken and all the remaining ingredients. Cook for 40 minutes on a low heat. Serve hot.

Chicken Curry with Eggs

Serves 4

Ingredients

6 garlic cloves

2.5cm/1in root ginger

25g/scant 1oz grated fresh coconut

2 tsp poppy seeds

1 tsp garam masala

1 tsp cumin seeds

1 tbsp coriander seeds

1 tsp turmeric

Salt to taste

4 tbsp refined vegetable oil

2 large onions, finely chopped

1kg/2¼lb chicken, chopped into 8 pieces

4 eggs, hard-boiled and halved

Method

- Grind together the garlic, ginger, coconut, poppy seeds, garam masala, cumin seeds, coriander seeds, turmeric and salt. Set aside.

- Heat the oil in a saucepan. Add the onions and the ground paste. Fry on a medium heat for 3-4 minutes. Add the chicken and mix well to coat.

- Simmer for 40 minutes. Garnish with the eggs and serve hot.

Chicken Fried with Spices

Ingredients
1kg/2¼lb chicken, chopped into 8 pieces

250ml/8fl oz refined vegetable oil

For the marinade:
1½ tsp ground coriander

4 green cardamom pods

7.5cm/3in cinnamon

½ tsp fennel seeds

1 tbsp garam masala

4-6 garlic cloves

2.5cm/1in root ginger

1 large onion, grated

1 large tomato, puréed

Salt to taste

Method

- Grind all the marinade ingredients together. Marinate the chicken with this mixture for 30 minutes.
- Cook the marinated chicken in a saucepan on a medium heat for 30 minutes, stirring occasionally.
- Heat the oil and fry the cooked chicken for 5-6 minutes. Serve hot.

Goan Kombdi

(Goan Chicken Curry)

Serves 4

Ingredients

1kg/2¼lb chicken, chopped into 8 pieces

Salt to taste

½ tsp turmeric

6 red chillies

5 cloves

5cm/2in cinnamon

1 tbsp coriander seeds

½ tsp fenugreek seeds

½ tsp mustard seeds

4 tbsp oil

1 tbsp tamarind paste

500ml/16fl oz coconut milk

Method

- Marinate the chicken with the salt and turmeric for 1 hour. Set aside.
- Grind together the chillies, cloves, cinnamon, coriander seeds, fenugreek seeds and mustard seeds with enough water to form a paste.
- Heat the oil in a saucepan. Fry the paste for 4 minutes. Add the chicken, tamarind paste and coconut milk. Simmer for 40 minutes and serve hot.

South Chicken Curry

Serves 4

Ingredients

16 cashew nuts

6 red chillies

2 tbsp coriander seeds

½ tsp cumin seeds

1 tbsp lemon juice

5 tbsp ghee

3 large onions, finely chopped

10 garlic cloves, finely chopped

2.5cm/1in root ginger, finely chopped

1kg/2¼lb chicken, chopped into 12 pieces

1 tsp turmeric

Salt to taste

500ml/16fl oz coconut milk

Method

- Grind the cashew nuts, red chillies, coriander seeds, cumin seeds and lemon juice with enough water to form a smooth paste. Set aside.
- Heat the ghee. Add the onions, garlic and ginger. Fry for 2 minutes.
- Add the chicken, turmeric, salt and the cashew nut paste. Fry for 5 minutes. Add the coconut milk and simmer for 40 minutes. Serve hot.

Nizami Chicken

(Chicken cooked with Saffron and Almonds)

Serves 4

Ingredients

4 tbsp refined vegetable oil

1 large chicken, chopped into 8 pieces

Salt to taste

750ml/1¼ pints milk

½ tsp saffron, soaked in 2 tsp milk

For the spice mixture:

1 tbsp ginger paste

3 tbsp poppy seeds

5 red chillies

25g/scant 1oz desiccated coconut

20 almonds

6 tbsp milk

Method

- Grind the spice mixture ingredients together to form a smooth paste.
- Heat the oil in a saucepan. Fry the paste on a low heat for 4 minutes.
- Add the chicken, salt and milk. Simmer for 40 minutes, stirring frequently. Add the saffron and simmer for another 5 minutes. Serve hot.

Duck Buffad

(Duck cooked with Vegetables)

Serves 4

Ingredients

4 tbsp ghee

3 large onions, quartered

750g/1lb 10oz duck, chopped into 8 pieces

3 large potatoes, quartered

50g/1¾oz cabbage, chopped

200g/7oz frozen peas

1 tsp turmeric

4 green chillies, slit lengthways

1 tsp ground cinnamon

1 tsp ground cloves

30g/1oz mint leaves, finely chopped

Salt to taste

750ml/1¼ pints water

1 tbsp malt vinegar

Method

- Heat the ghee in a saucepan. Add the onions and fry on a medium heat till brown. Add the duck and sauté for 5-6 minutes.
- Add the remaining ingredients, except the water and vinegar. Fry for 8 minutes. Add the water and vinegar. Simmer for 40 minutes. Serve hot.

Adraki Murgh

(Ginger Chicken)

Serves 4

Ingredients

2 tbsp refined vegetable oil

2 large onions, finely chopped

2 tbsp ginger paste

½ tsp garlic paste

½ tsp turmeric

1 tbsp garam masala

1 tomato, finely chopped

1kg/2¼lb chicken, chopped into 12 pieces

Salt to taste

Method

- Heat the oil in a saucepan. Add the onions, ginger paste and garlic paste and fry on a medium heat for 1-2 minutes.
- Add all the remaining ingredients and sauté for 5-6 minutes.
- Grill the mixture for 40 minutes and serve hot.

Bharva Murgh

(Stuffed Chicken)

Serves 4

Ingredients

½ tsp ginger paste

½ tsp garlic paste

1 tsp tamarind paste

1kg/2¼lb chicken

75g/2½oz ghee

2 large onions, finely chopped

Salt to taste

3 large potatoes, chopped

2 tsp ground coriander

1 tsp ground cumin

1 tsp mustard powder

50g/1¾oz coriander leaves, chopped

2 cloves

2.5cm/1in cinnamon

Method

- Mix the ginger, garlic and tamarind pastes. Marinate the chicken with the mixture for 3 hours. Set aside.
- Heat the ghee in a saucepan and fry the onions till brown. Add all the remaining ingredients, except the marinated chicken. Fry for 6 minutes.
- Stuff this mixture into the marinated chicken. Roast in an oven at 190°C (375°F, Gas Mark 5) for 45 minutes. Serve hot.

Malaidar Murgh

(Chicken cooked in Creamy Gravy)

Serves 4

Ingredients

4 tbsp refined vegetable oil

2 large onions, finely chopped

¼ tsp ground cloves

Salt to taste

1kg/2¼lb chicken, chopped into 12 pieces

250ml/8fl oz water

3 tomatoes, finely chopped

125g/4½oz yoghurt, whisked

500ml/16fl oz single cream

2 tbsp cashew nuts, ground

10g/¼oz coriander leaves, chopped

Method

- Heat the oil in a saucepan. Add the onions, cloves and salt. Fry on a medium heat for 3 minutes. Add the chicken and sauté for 7-8 minutes.
- Add the water and tomatoes. Cook for 30 minutes.
- Add the yoghurt, cream and cashew nuts. Simmer for 10 minutes.
- Garnish with the coriander leaves and serve hot.

Bombay Chicken Curry

Serves 4

Ingredients

8 tbsp refined vegetable oil

1kg/2¼lb chicken, chopped into 12 pieces

2 large onions, sliced

1 tsp ginger paste

1 tsp garlic paste

4 cloves, ground

2.5cm/1in cinnamon, ground

1 tsp ground cumin

Salt to taste

2 tomatoes, finely chopped

500ml/16fl oz water

Method

- Heat half the oil in a frying pan. Add the chicken and fry on a medium heat for 5-6 minutes. Set aside.
- Heat the remaining oil in a saucepan. Add the onions, ginger paste and garlic paste and fry on a medium heat till the onions turn brown. Add the remaining ingredients, except the water and chicken. Sauté for 5-6 minutes.
- Add the fried chicken and water. Simmer for 30 minutes and serve hot.

Durbari Chicken

(Rich Gravy Chicken)

Serves 4

Ingredients

150g/5½oz chana dhal*

Salt to taste

1 litre/1¾ pints water

2.5cm/1in root ginger

10 garlic cloves

4 red chillies

3 tbsp ghee

2 large onions, finely chopped

½ tsp turmeric

2 tbsp garam masala

½ tbsp poppy seeds

2 tomatoes, finely chopped

1kg/2¼lb chicken, chopped into 10-12 pieces

2 tsp tamarind paste

20 cashew nuts, ground to a paste

250ml/8fl oz water

250ml/8fl oz coconut milk

Method

- Mix the dhal with salt and half the water. Cook in a saucepan on a medium heat for 45 minutes. Grind to a paste with the ginger, garlic and red chillies.
- Heat the ghee in a saucepan. Add the onions, dhal mixture and turmeric. Fry on a medium heat for 3-4 minutes. Add all the remaining ingredients.
- Mix well and simmer for 40 minutes, stirring occasionally. Serve hot.

Duck Fry

Serves 4

Ingredients

3 tbsp malt vinegar

2 tbsp ground coriander

½ tsp ground black pepper

Salt to taste

1kg/2¼lb duck, chopped into 8 pieces

60ml/2fl oz refined vegetable oil

2 small onions

1 litre/1¾ pints hot water

Method

- Mix the vinegar with the ground coriander, pepper and salt. Marinate the duck with this mixture for 1 hour.
- Heat the oil in a saucepan. Fry the onions on a medium heat till brown.
- Add the water, salt and the duck. Simmer for 45 minutes and serve hot.

Coriander Garlic Chicken

Serves 4

Ingredients

4 tbsp refined vegetable oil

5cm/2in cinnamon

3 green cardamom pods

4 cloves

2 bay leaves

3 large onions, finely chopped

10 garlic cloves, finely chopped

1 tsp ginger paste

3 tomatoes, finely chopped

1 large chicken, chopped

250ml/8fl oz water

150g/5½oz coriander leaves, chopped

Salt to taste

Method

- Heat the oil in a saucepan. Add the cinnamon, cardamom, cloves, bay leaves, onions, garlic and ginger paste. Fry for 2-3 minutes.
- Add all the remaining ingredients. Simmer for 40 minutes and serve hot.

Masala Duck

Ingredients

30g/1oz ghee plus 1 tbsp for frying

1 large onion, finely sliced

1 tsp ginger paste

1 tsp garlic paste

1 tsp ground coriander

½ tsp ground black pepper

1 tsp turmeric

1kg/2¼lb duck, chopped into 12 pieces

1 tbsp malt vinegar

Salt to taste

5cm/2in cinnamon

3 cloves

1 tsp mustard seeds

Method

- Heat 30g/1oz of the ghee in a saucepan. Add the onion, ginger paste, garlic paste, coriander, pepper and turmeric. Fry for 6 minutes.
- Add the duck. Fry on a medium heat for 5 minutes. Add the vinegar and salt. Mix well and simmer for 40 minutes. Set aside.
- Heat the remaining ghee in a saucepan and add the cinnamon, cloves and mustard seeds. Let them splutter for 15 seconds. Pour this over the duck mixture and serve hot.

Mustard Chicken

Serves 4

Ingredients

2 large tomatoes, finely chopped

10g/¼oz mint leaves, finely chopped

30g/1oz coriander leaves, chopped

2.5cm/1in root ginger, peeled

8 garlic cloves

3 tbsp mustard oil

2 tsp mustard seeds

½ tsp fenugreek seeds

1kg/2¼lb chicken, chopped into 12 pieces

500ml/16fl oz warm water

Salt to taste

Method

- Grind the tomatoes, mint leaves, coriander leaves, ginger and garlic to a smooth paste. Set aside.
- Heat the oil in a saucepan. Add the mustard seeds and fenugreek seeds. Let them splutter for 15 seconds.
- Add the tomato paste and fry on a medium heat for 2-3 minutes. Add the chicken, water and salt. Mix well and simmer for 40 minutes. Serve hot.

Murgh Lassanwallah

(Garlic Chicken)

Serves 4

Ingredients

400g/14oz yoghurt

3 tsp garlic paste

1½ tsp garam masala

Salt to taste

750g/1lb 10oz boneless chicken, chopped into 12 pieces

1 tbsp refined vegetable oil

1 tsp cumin seeds

25g/scant 1oz dill leaves

500ml/16fl oz milk

1 tbsp ground black pepper

Method

- Mix the yoghurt, garlic paste, garam masala and salt together. Marinate the chicken with this mixture for 10-12 hours.
- Heat the oil. Add the cumin seeds and let them splutter for 15 seconds. Add the marinated chicken and fry on a medium heat for 20 minutes.
- Add the dill leaves, milk and pepper. Simmer for 15 minutes. Serve hot.

Pepper Chicken Chettinad

(South Indian Pepper Chicken)

Serves 4

Ingredients

2½ tbsp refined vegetable oil

10 curry leaves

3 large onions, finely chopped

1 tsp ginger paste

1 tsp garlic paste

½ tsp turmeric

2 tomatoes, finely chopped

½ tsp ground fennel seeds

¼ tsp ground cloves

500ml/16fl oz water

1kg/2¼lb chicken, chopped into 12 pieces

Salt to taste

1½ tsp coarsely ground black pepper

Method

- Heat the oil in a saucepan. Add the curry leaves, onions, ginger paste and garlic paste. Fry on a medium heat for a minute.
- Add all the remaining ingredients. Simmer for 40 minutes and serve hot.

Chicken Mince with Eggs

Serves 4

Ingredients

3 tbsp refined vegetable oil

4 eggs, hard-boiled and sliced

2 large onions, finely chopped

2 tsp ginger paste

2 tsp garlic paste

2 tomatoes, finely chopped

1 tsp ground cumin

2 tsp ground coriander

½ tsp turmeric

8-10 curry leaves

1 tsp garam masala

750g/1lb 10oz chicken, minced

Salt to taste

360ml/12fl oz water

Method

- Heat the oil in a saucepan. Add the eggs. Fry for 2 minutes and set aside.
- To the same oil, add the onions, ginger paste and garlic paste. Fry on a medium heat for 2-3 minutes.
- Add all the remaining ingredients, except the water. Mix well and fry for 5 minutes. Add the water. Simmer for 30 minutes.
- Garnish with the eggs. Serve hot.

Dry Chicken

Ingredients

1kg/2¼lb chicken, chopped into 12 pieces

6 tbsp refined vegetable oil

3 large onions, thinly sliced

For the marinade:

8 red chillies

1 tbsp sesame seeds

1 tbsp coriander seeds

1 tsp garam masala

4 green cardamom pods

10 garlic cloves

3.5cm/1½in root ginger

6 tbsp malt vinegar

Salt to taste

Method

- Grind all the marinade ingredients together to a smooth paste. Marinate the chicken with this paste for 3 hours.
- Heat the oil in a saucepan. Fry the onions on a low heat till brown. Add the chicken and cook for 40 minutes, stirring frequently. Serve hot.

Lightning Source UK Ltd.
Milton Keynes UK
UKHW022017190421
382278UK00003B/593